Billy went up to the top of the hill.

Billy went bump, bump, bump to the bottom of the hill.

Tom went up to the top of the hill.

Tom went bump, bump, bump to the bottom of the hill.

Billy and Tom play at the bottom of the hill.

The big pig went up to the top of the hill.

The big pig went BUMP, BUMP, BUMP to the bottom of the hill.

Billy and Tom play with dad at the bottom of the hill.